EMPOWERED

2022

BREAK THE CHAINS

Edited By Wendy Laws

First published in Great Britain in 2022 by:

 Young**Writers**®
— Est. 1991 —

Young Writers
Remus House
Coltsfoot Drive
Peterborough
PE2 9BF
Telephone: 01733 890066
Website: www.youngwriters.co.uk

Printed and bound in the UK by BookPrintingUK
Website: www.bookprintinguk.com
YB0510M

⭐ FOREWORD ⭐

Since 1991, here at Young Writers we have celebrated the awesome power of creative writing, especially in young adults where it can serve as a vital method of expressing their emotions and views about the world around them. In every poem we see the effort and thought that each student published in this book has put into their work and by creating this anthology we hope to encourage them further with the ultimate goal of sparking a life-long love of writing.

Our latest competition for secondary school students, Empowered, challenged young writers to consider what was important to them. We wanted to give them a voice, the chance to express themselves freely and honestly, something which is so important for these young adults to feel confident and listened to. They could give an opinion, share a memory, consider a dilemma, impart advice or simply write about something they love. There were no restrictions on style or subject so you will find an anthology brimming with a variety of poetic styles and topics. We hope you find it as absorbing as we have.

We encourage young writers to express themselves and address subjects that matter to them, which sometimes means writing about sensitive or contentious topics. If you have been affected by any issues raised in this book, details on where to find help can be found at www.youngwriters.co.uk/info/other/contact-lines

⭐ CONTENTS ⭐

Ruya Calili (11) 61
Sianna Dimitrova (12) 62
Kalifa Dennis (11) 63
Josie Julie Knight (11) 64
Lucy Holmes (12) 65
Darcy Wilson (12) 66
Loreta Fana (12) 67
Rosie Hutler (13) 68
Jack Avanzi (11) 69
Tayla Walton (12) 70
Desharna Bailey-Hanley (12) 71
Farhan Mahmood (12) 72
Josh Terumalai (13) 73
Jessica Lupu (13) 74
Yuhua Wang (12) 75
Dylan Aslan (13) 76
Emir Boztepe (11) 77
Vanesa Lwanga (13) 78
Aisha Cogliandro (13) 79
Ava Allison (11) 80
Ashirah Defroand (13) 81
Maryam Asid (12) 82
Talia Edwards (12) 83
April Foley (12) 84
Buse Boran (13) 85
Ashton Alvarez (12) 86
Ayla Candaner (11) 87
Ilir Gashi (12) 88
Paige Stein (12) 89
Mairah Asghar (11) 90
Kezia Amedume (13) 91
Ryan Thomson (12) 92
Rosie Keuning (12) 93
Sofia Halacheva (12) 94
Mason Steck (12) 95

Hyndland Secondary School, Hyndland

Nafsica Ladas (15) 96

Mulberry UTC, Bow

Darbie Veness (17) 97

Ormiston Beachcroft Academy, London

Frankie Hudson-Green 98
Oren Gerald-Williams (11) 99
Ali Rida (11) 100
Rezan Muhammed (16) 101
Tariq Noor 102
Seysha 103
Masood Ridha 104

Parrs Wood High School, East Didsbury

Roj Almohammad (14) 105
Aminah Ajala-Edwards (14) 106
Abubakar Bhatti (13) 108
Abbas Kazemi (12) 110
Bilal Hussain (13) 112
Cheuk Tung Lui (13) 114

Ratcliffe College, Ratcliffe On The Wreake

Sophia Alexander (12) 115

Regent High School, Camden

Tania Begum (13) 116

Rockport School, Craigavad

Isaac Noblett (13) 117

Sir Robert Pattinson Academy, North Hykeham

Olivia Andrews (13) 118
William Kearns (12) 120
Phoebe Wilson (11) 121
Ellie Dalton (12) 122
Taya Garrard (13) 123

Jayden Brewer (13)   198

Wollaston School, Wollaston

Tazmin Maarman (12)   199

THE POEMS

My Battle, My Future

I fight
When I cannot breathe.
When my lungs constrict
Under the weight of an anaconda.

I break
The bell rings
I shake
I cannot do this.

I boil
To a breaking point
My body floods with anxiety
I come to school
Just to leave again.

I'm scared
The help I need
Waiting for me
You'll get me through this
I can do this.

I'm healing
I still shake, I still break
But, I pick myself up
Fighting for another day.

Rachael Bell (17)
Annan Academy, Annan

Children Should Be Heard, Not Seen

Suffering in silence,
Because they're too frightened to say anything.
Suffering in silence,
Because they're scared no one will believe them.
Suffering in silence,
Because the judge won't listen.
Suffering in silence,
Because they can't escape.

But we refuse to keep quiet,
We will speak the truth.
Loud enough to cause an avalanche,
Loud enough to break free,
From the cage that contains us.

Neve Nicholson (13)
Annan Academy, Annan

The Butterfly

Splash!
A raindrop landed on a butterfly's wings
Muddy, grubby, and all sorts of things
She was now stuck in a puddle
When all she wanted was her mum's cuddle.

The rain slowly turned into a storm
The butterfly's wings began to be torn
Struggling, fighting, wanting to rise
She found herself helpless, closing her eyes.

She was thinking of her young, carefree, innocent life
Which she may never get back
Amid this strife.

Where is my freedom?
Where is my liberty?
Will I just be thrown into the bitter sea?
And just before she lost all her hope
A little ray of light she could see elope.

Her wings started to feel lighter
The sun shone brighter
The raindrops rolled down her tiny, fragile body
And even though she was still muddy
Light sparkled at the end of the tunnel
And her joy was exceptional.

Zita Warren (12)
Arts & Media School, Islington

YaadGaar Incident

"Flight attendants, prepare for take-off please."
The death angels are getting ready.
A man to ask - salute to you, champ!
T, t, t, tuh, the propellers roaring,
Leaving the beloved city like a lion without the worry of his life.
Into the air, you go, 'the Beatle of Pakistan'.
Another step and you're the one.
You can do it, from Chitral to Islamabad,
Like an eagle - the legend of the beloved.
You have failed to fly, you are a murderer.
Kaboom! Dropped like a martyr who has achieved his target,
The bow's arrow has hit the bullseye!
The hot air acting like the cold air, *swoosh*,
The roar of the wind, the lightning of the dark clouds, the constant rain of arrows.
Oh! Jamshed has died! Oh, Jamshed has died!
Brain, you have failed to keep the bird in the air.
"Oh, 'Shaheen', what have you done?"
How could you?
You have sentenced trillions of people to death or have you?
I guess you have.
The martyrs have passed the mission!
Passed the exam,
The big question is, are the results here?

Are they?
Jamshed joins,
'Jannat' reaching his points.

The news is spreading like wildfire!
Such a nice man,
The heart of gold, the hope of many people,
The angels are here, his death is a solved mystery!
Jamshed the legend.
My legend.

Muhammad Dawood (13)
Arts & Media School, Islington

Reflection

Mirror, mirror on the wall,
I see someone I've never met before,
The woman with burnt leaf eyes I adore,
The woman with a voice,
A voice so inspiring and powerful,
Her throat was so parched and sore,
The woman said, "I'm you,
I'm the one you ignore."
She's right, how can I be pure?
Rays of sun pierce my skin,
The window whistled,
The spark in me twinkled and glowed,
Confidence a song I could repeat,
Respect a shadow that reflects when I speak,
Not the best scholar,
But I'm still a part of AMSI,
The emerald pool flows in my veins,
Yet I have a voice in me,
I'm Dominican not republican,
That's the confidence inside of me,
The woman with the burnt leaf eyes,
She's a part of me.

Rayah Laudat (13)
Arts & Media School, Islington

Your Future

People hurt each other.
Why? I don't know.
That's how history went
And how it still goes.

Tied down, thrown around,
Opinions lost in this populated crowd.
But we still have to march forward,
Like soldiers - Battle of Fulford.

But it doesn't have to be this way,
Despite our lives being delayed,
Don't let your opinions be swayed,
Don't be drowned by a sea of hate.

Your future is yours
Not mine to debate.
Don't let people bring you down,
You lead your future like an invisible crown.

So when someone else starts to fall,
Remind them that it's all worth it after all.

Cherlaé Brown-Richards (11)
Arts & Media School, Islington

Change

Be the change you wish to see,
The person you aspire to be,
The person who changes the world,
The person who makes a difference,
That person could be you.

Change is different,
Change is scary,
But change is what helps us grow,
Change may help you to let go.

Life is hard,
Life is strange,
Cry sometimes,
Don't just be brave.

Live life as yourself,
Don't go to any length to be someone else,
Or told you can't do something new,
Just be you.

Empower others,
Empower yourself,
Don't let others control your opinions
Or who you are or wish to be,
Just be you.

Blaise Arbuckle (11)
Arts & Media School, Islington

Me

You don't know my entire story yet you think you can destroy me, thinking you know everything about me, bullying me and verbally abusing me.

You don't know my entire story yet you bully me for who I am, calling me an improper bus enthusiast because of a simple bus route.

You know what I look like, you know what routes I like, you also know what I make but here's a fact that you didn't know about me, I am confident, motivated, I'm a human like you, I am creative, a gamer, a human like you.

Is my opinion so offensive?

You guys always judge me for it.

Is my opinion so offensive?

Why are you treating me like a guinea pig that is very weak?

Alesha Henry (13)
Arts & Media School, Islington

The Fight

Midstride, molten flame
Not every soldier feels the pain
Stumbling terror
Rifle sweating
Everybody yelling

Crackling dynamite
And a call of a name
When will our government pull the reign?

As a group, we make our way up
Not knowing about the shell
That's about to make us all duck

Man on man
That's how we fight
We know it's not right;
It's not out of spite

Bullets firing
Many men dying
Whilst our leaders
Are at home, making something to eat
Maybe something's frying?
All whilst another soldier is dying.

Jason Edwin
Arts & Media School, Islington

Exhale

The humans say I'm beautiful
And that my colours shine,
Then why do they drain this colour of mine?
Boom! The sound of trees falling to the ground
You go, "I want to be next," as I listen to the sound.
Every day breathing gets harder, I think I will fail.
Inhale, exhale.
I used to bloom and blossom.
The humans would gasp and gape when they saw me.
Now all I am is a pointless plant.
Now my petals wilt, now will humans feel guilt?
Inhale, exhale.
My stem droops like it's trying to meet my roots.
Dehydration. Hallucination.
Inhale, exhale.

Eliza Suruk (12)
Arts & Media School, Islington

Wake Up To Reality

Wake up to reality!
Nothing ever goes as planned in this accursed world.
The longer you live, the more you realise that the only things that truly exist in this reality are merely pain, suffering and futility.
Listen, everywhere you look in this world, wherever there is light, there will always be shadows to be found as well.
As long as there is a concept of victors,
the vanquished will also exist.
The selfish intent of wanting to preserve peace initiates war and hatred is born in order to protect loved ones.
There are nexuses, casual relationships that cannot be separated.

Amir Salehi (12)
Arts & Media School, Islington

Fragile Soul

She was faint-hearted and couldn't trust
In result of all the lies she'd been told
All the myths that didn't exist
But still pushed her to take the risk.

The risks that weren't worth the fight
The fight that wasn't worth the struggle
She proceeded as she was told not to give up
But unfortunately, she had no luck.

After she'd comprehended what had happened
Deleted things about what they had said
Her trust issues were out of control
Her feelings were cracked like an old porcelain doll
Finally another fragile soul.

Shantae Gardner (11)
Arts & Media School, Islington

Dear Rose

Dear Rose,
One thing I tell you,
You are as my gift,
Like if you were my grandmother,
Rosa.

Dear Rose,
You are my inspiration,
You are like her name,
You are like my grandmother,
Her name is Rosa,
My grandmother is Rosa.

Dear Rose,
You are a field, with flowers
Of colours,
You are beautiful, like my grandmother.
Rosa.

Dear Rose,
Flower of the earth,
You are beautiful, and you are the best,
You are silvery red,
Her name is Rose, like my grandmother Rosa.

Lytzi Franco (11)
Arts & Media School, Islington

Family

My family is wonderful,
Each one of us is respectful,
With lots of love and care,
Household chores we share.

Long-distance family members
We rarely see, every other December,
Yet our love for each other
No one can question and nothing can compare.

We sometimes quarrel and fight
But respect is always on sight,
And in our gloomy nights
There are always sparks of light.

Family from Philippines,
Family from Algeria,
I will visit them soon,
They are all courteous and superior.

Shayma Mezrig (11)
Arts & Media School, Islington

Believe

It's all over, you believe
Your mind is a distressed jungle
And you want to smile but break into a sigh
You think you're all alone, nestled in your thoughts

Life is boisterous with its highs and lows
The harder you try you will reach your goals
Perfect no one has been to know
Do not give up though velocity may seem slow

Listen, I want you to know
You're a prodigious person, just let time slow
Fight when you are hardest hit
It's when things seem inadequate that you must not quit.

Amina Mohamed (11)
Arts & Media School, Islington

Advice - Poem To My Younger Self

To my younger self
If I could say one thing
You're truly never alone
You are cared for like me right now
Thank you very much for getting me where I am today
Look after yourself/myself
I'm proud of you.

If you fall down
Get up and don't stay on the ground
If you didn't achieve
What you want to be
Try again to be steadfast and free
Be free from your weakness and fears
If you try
You will say goodbye
To the fears
And that is how
Practice makes perfect.

Ralph Tan (12)
Arts & Media School, Islington

Boxing

Bang!
That's the sound that the boxing bag
Makes when it's been hit.
Sweat and blood is a sight
On people's faces.
Vaseline on the side of the
People with huge cuts on
Their faces.

The sound of people falling onto
The ground because of defeat.
People cheating and some people
Crying in disbelief.

The sight of sweat
Falling off the faces of people
That are getting punched in the face.
The sound of people crashing
To the ground.

Justin Francis (11)
Arts & Media School, Islington

You Can

If you think you can do it, you can
If you think you can't do it, you can't
If you think you will lose, you're lost
Always try your best.

It's easier than it seems
It may be near when it seems so far
When things seem bad, don't lose your hope
One day you're as bright as a star
You know what others may never know.

You can learn from your mistakes
Don't say tomorrow, do it all today
The time can be short
Don't leave things undone.

Ezana Yirgalem (12)
Arts & Media School, Islington

From The Future

Dear past me,
Enjoy outside to the fullest
In a couple of years Covid-19 will come
And you will be put in lockdown with limited things to do.

Dear past me,
Secondary will be like hell
So don't take primary for granted
Trust me, it gets worse and the teachers will still despise
you.

Dear past me,
Live life how you want
You will end up getting into a nice life if you do
Don't force yourself to do something you don't want to do,
even if someone tells you.

Mikel Thomas (12)
Arts & Media School, Islington

What Makes Me Me

What makes me me
is what people don't see.
People don't decide
what you want to be,
by your fantasies.
You decide what you want to be,
not the mirrors reflecting hate.

They say you have to be like them.
They try to change you and break you,
but it won't work.

I will take off the mask
and show them who I am.

Peyton Burgess (11)
Arts & Media School, Islington

Night-Time

Oh, starry sky,
I stand on my balcony
and wish I could fly,
staring at the silent sight
of the starry sky.

How many frosted specks fill a dark black place?
All that's heard is the soft, soft wind,
oh, night-time skies, what a wonderful place.

The night-time sky,
shining like silver,
but as dark as the Devil's heart.

Indio Brown (12)
Arts & Media School, Islington

Prime Minister For A Day

If I was prime minister for a day,
It would be a great day,
People having fun,
Playing all day.

If I was prime minister for a day,
No school,
Just all games,
Just for a day.

If I was prime minister for a day,
It would be no working hard,
Or draining energy on school,
Just if I were prime minister for a day.

Tyler Addey (13)
Arts & Media School, Islington

To My Future Self

Dear future me,
all I ask from you is
to follow your dreams,
don't let them get to you,
even though they might not go,
ignore them, pursue your dreams.

Dear future me,
all I ask from you is
please, please, please
get good grades
and please get a good job,
this is all I ask from you,
good luck.

Leonardo Dias Barreto (12)
Arts & Media School, Islington

24

I Am The Sword

I am the sword big and mighty.
I am the sword, the fighting tool of man.
I am sharp and shiny, the frontline tool.
I am the sword, destroyer of man.
I am a weapon, I am a shield.
I am the delivered of and the deliverer from death.
I am the sword, swift, clean and final.

Kahdel Neunie-Osimen (12)
Arts & Media School, Islington

Dear Mum

When things were rough
we would make it through.
You gave me a home and for all of that
I want to say thank you.
When I cried, you would wipe my tears.
When I wanted to give up,
you would help me and tell me to try my best.
and for that, I want to say thank you.

Angel Dixon (12)
Arts & Media School, Islington

Message To Self

B　e the best you can be
I　magine what you can do
R　emember who you are
T　here's nobody who doesn't like you
H　onour your past
D　well on your heart
A　ll you need is love
Y　our birthday is the start.

Krystal Brennan Bonaparte (11)

Arts & Media School, Islington

I Am Sad

I am sad
I cannot do anything good
And I am bad
At everything and mostly when I am tired
When I take time to do things
It never works like I want it to, so I always leave the place
I am so sad, I am so bad and never will be good.

Iker Gonzalez
Arts & Media School, Islington

Alone

One day, one adventure,
Sitting under a tree,
Calm, reading a book,
No one to talk with,
Dark day, dark emotions,
Alone and bored,
Writing this poem for you.

Adriana Romero (12)
Arts & Media School, Islington

The Truth From The Liars

No self-expression, it's against the rules but to express
yourself you need to learn who you are;
Enjoy your childhood while it's still here but grow up
because adulthood isn't far;
Go after what you want in life but don't want for less when
you could have more;
Live life as you wish to live it but you must obey the rules of
a world before;
Bullying is not tolerated but they are immature, they will
learn;
You will control the future but if you don't fix the past the
world will burn;
What is taught is the truth but it's manipulated into what
we wanted;
Growing up is tiring but you don't have time to be
exhausted;
You know the new world better than most but you still
haven't adjusted;
The government and the police protect you but they cannot
be trusted;
Know yourself and your identity but we will not educate;
We want to give you your best chance but to you, we will
prevaricate;
Stand up if treated wrongly but don't dare to try to fight;
Nobody knows everything but your elders are always right;
Enjoy the life you have but you have to lead the next
generation;

Your mental health is our main focus but what's important is your education;
Listen to what we say but don't, all we do is contradict;
But of course, this is something that no one could predict;
Because if they are meant to teach us how to live and be polite;
They would tell us the truth, right? Right?

Scarlett Cooper (15)

Cansfield High School, Ashton-In-Makerfield

Bowl Of Identity

A bowl of identity,
Unequal and unmatched,
Although completely mixed,
The servings are unbalanced,
Both brown and white sugar,
Needed for mixture,
Yet white is greater weighted,
For no reason but preference.
Drops of colour,
All choose how to blend,
Yet overpowered and dictated by the
Flour, they work with the egg yolk,
Each gain from the other on a personal level.
No dependence on others,
No care for the others.
Time for the oven,
To secure their decisions,
Not ready to bake,
But not ready for change,
When all is done.
The cake is uneven,
Disgusting and bleak,
Too late for a do-over,
Cover it up,

However thick the icing becomes
The old work shines through,
What's has been done can't be undone,
Only reshaped and rethought.

Emma Wilkinson (16)
Cansfield High School, Ashton-In-Makerfield

Friends

F riends support you and help you
R ecommend ideas
I ndicate your weaknesses
E very day they are there to support you
N o matter what situation
D o things with you, help you
S upport you when you're down.

Jonathan Grundy (12)
Cansfield High School, Ashton-In-Makerfield

Empower Yourself

It's a fine artwork of lush greenery and scenery, there is joy.
It's nature at its finest and oh, it's at its most divine.
The water filled with koi fish makes you want to wish it stays like this but alas the world is cruel, they create laws, conventions and rules.
They create clouds of smoke making animals choke.
They soak the mind with malice-filled potions,
They kill all animals inside the ocean.
However, some people are kind and good-hearted,
They treat the animals with a soothing lotion.
They make the world seem caring and warm.
They give us kindness and motivation,
The kindness and motivation we need to help all people and animals through.
Plants as well, to save them from the axe which does devilish acts.
Acts that if carried out to a certain extent will kill us all.
Animals and plants as well so I suggest,
We empower ourselves and stop these crimes.

Abdul Enus (11)
Hatch End High School, Hatch End

In Every Sweep

With every sweep children cry,
Smoke crawling up the chimney,
With every cough people die,
Their bodies pale and skinny.

With every laugh from the rich,
Comes a scream from the poor,
Workers and children thrown in a ditch,
And being completely ignored.

Men and children being exploited,
But to the establishment, no fingers pointed,
Every day more people losing faith in churches,
The news about the industrial revolution is heard in crowds,
then disperses.

People on the street inspired by the French revolution
Stories of how the French stood up, demanded an execution
It's too late, children have turned to a life of prostitution
To fix London now, why there's no solution.

Amel El-Hasnaoui (12)
Hatch End High School, Hatch End

Everyone Is Equal

Everyone is equal,
No matter what or who you are.
The pathway is not far.
Be proud of yourself!

Everyone is equal,
No matter the race,
No matter the face.
You're human.

Everyone is equal,
Doesn't matter if you have a disability or an illness.
You still have an ability!
Be yourself! You're amazing!

Everyone is equal,
If you get picked on,
Stand up for yourself!
Don't let anyone not let you be yourself.

Everyone is equal.
Be confident,
Speak up!
Don't be shy because that's not who you are.
We're all equal.

Aysha Zubair (11)
Hatch End High School, Hatch End

My Powerful Mum

My mum is the best, do you know why?
Well, because she just is.
When I was about six or seven years old,
I was at this running competition,
I was running with girls a year above me,
The race started and the girls zoomed off in front of me
And I was behind all of them, then *boom!*
My mum was shouting, "You've got this."
That somehow made me feel stronger,
She kept on shouting that out.
Every time she did I started running faster and faster
Until it was the end of the race.
Starting last, then ending second,
Someone still got first.
My mum is the best!

Nikita Soukup (12)
Hatch End High School, Hatch End

I Love Christmas

I love Christmas, it is the best
Everybody, wake up, no time to rest.
I love Christmas, it is the best
Oh wait, I forgot, I have to get dressed
I love Christmas, it is the best
But I always thought Santa lives in the west
I love Christmas, it is the best
I think I got what I wanted, I'm not sure, I just guessed
I love Christmas, it is the best
I got so many presents, I have been blessed
I love Christmas, it is the best
Now there is time to finally rest.

Shay Halai (11)
Hatch End High School, Hatch End

Slavery

Children working with their blood and sweat,
As they're getting upset,
Coming to this church was a regret,
But they tend to forgive and forget.

Children working with their blood and sweat,
Then there comes a laugh from the rich,
The children hope they fall in a ditch,
Because they're truly a witch,
But then there goes a snitch.

Faith Ofosu-Agyapong (11)
Hatch End High School, Hatch End

You're Not Alone

Everyone has days where they feel alone,
but a little bit of motivation is all they might need.
Most people hide their thoughts, hide their feelings
or don't speak out, afraid of people's judgements.
Power people through their hardest times,
support and reassure them, anything to help them rise.
Old or young, you can still make a change, anyone can.
Whether it's a Monday or a Saturday, a rainy day
or a sunny day, make it your best day.
Every day is something new, make use of that.
Relatable and reliable, a type of person everyone needs in
their life.
Motivation, it comes in many forms,
it might seem like nothing but it gets you far.
Expectation is reality, you don't always have to compare
yourself to people on the internet, know your self-worth.
Never stop trying, giving up gets you nowhere so believe in
yourself.
Together we can face all challenges, all we have to do is
empower each other.

Sarah Bindas (13)
Heathcote School, Chingford

Remember, Transition Will Affect Me Differently From You

Transition, it happened to me.
Before I remember,
A baby in arms and then freely moving around the floor.
Transition will affect me differently from you.

Transition, it happened to me.
I don't remember much.
My parents split up,
Living in one house to two houses.
Transition will affect me differently from you.

Transition, it happened to me.
Bit older now,
Began to talk,
Joined nursery, a new environment I didn't know.
Remember, transition will affect me differently from you.

Transition, it happened to me.
Started primary school at the age of four.
Numbers, letters, I learnt it all,
Transitioning through the years until Year Five.
Remember, transition will affect me differently from you.

Transition, it happened to me.
Once we made it to Year Five, the whole world was stuck inside.
Zoom became the new classroom.
We made it through and then Year Six ended,
It was time to say goodbye.
Remember, transition will affect me differently from you.

Transition, it happened to me.
Started secondary school,
A new building, new friends, and a new way of learning,
Remember, transition will affect me differently from you.

Transition, it will continue to happen to me!

Freddie Stirling (11)
Heathcote School, Chingford

Feel Lucky With Ralph The Rabbit

Ralph the rabbit has an important job,
Growing up to fill his ancestors' shoes,
He's a tester, you know, you know the sort,
If only he knew what he had to do,
Feel lucky with what you've got because if only you knew...

Today's the day,
Ralph's 'exciting job'.
He has so much to say,
He doesn't know where to start,
When he arrived, he looked around,
It was an amazing lab
With lots of zap sounds,
Feel lucky with what you've got because if only you knew...

He was grabbed recklessly
And strapped to a chair.
"I'm a little rabbit," he said,
"Not a hare.
Argh!" he screamed. "Argh!" for his life
As a toxic liquid was syringed in his eye.
"You're all done." They hushed him away,
Bandaged up in tremendous pain.

Be lucky with what you've got,
The privileges in life,
When other living things are wasted
And tossed on by to die.
Be lucky with what you've got
And put a stop to things that aren't right.
Animal testing.

Olivia Clark (11)
Heathcote School, Chingford

We Are Told...

We are told when we are young,
that they like us because they
don't stop harassing us
the world was taught to embrace that.

We are told to watch out as we grow older
like it's our fault.
My brother is told to enjoy his day.
I'm told to look out for dark streets, stairwells.
Don't wear short skirts.
Don't show your shoulders.

Yet when it happens,
because all girls are sure it will,
we are told to speak out,
speak out, but not like that,
you're being dramatic,
you're blaming all men.
So if I blame the wrongdoer
then I'm blaming you all
so it's my fault
for being... free!

So don't shy away from the topic,
then maybe we can stop it.

Stop seeing girls as an object,
is she too young to wear that
or too young to be sexualized?
So maybe they can be free,
away from the restraints of their confinement
so they... aren't a... target.

Darcey Rudrum (12)
Heathcote School, Chingford

Success, Fear And Failure!

Success comes when you try, but it also comes when you fail
But people's world perspective narrates something else.
Failure is good. But is suffocated by fear. Why fear?
A four-letter word wrecks someone's brain,
It's like the sky falling and crumbling on the way.
'The only thing to fear is fear itself!'
So why fear?
Fear is a small emotion that grows inside you.
It wraps its small body around you and strangles every
single emotion.
The only way to conquer fear is to fail!
Failure is as dark as an abandoned tunnel.
But, there is always light at the end of the tunnel.
You might not see it, but, failure is not the end... only the
start!
You don't need to see the whole staircase just to take the
first step!
Because taking that first step, you might just find success.

Rufaro Macheka (13)
Heathcote School, Chingford

48

Yellow Stars

Running,
Screaming,
Shouting.

Panting like wild dogs in desperation to seek refuge.
At that very moment, the train roared past us like a flying
dragon.
They didn't care about us, we had to go at the back of a
wagon.

I thought the world was full of variety,
As we went down the ladder of society.
Yellow stars were on our coats but they didn't define me -
I am Anne Frank!

Chucked in the concentration camps, as if we were rubbish
With little food to share, but at this point in time,
I was just glad to be alive!

In April 1945, our dismal lives were full of hope again,
The trees blossomed a beautiful pink,
The trees were full of hope and love - the children began to
laugh again.

In life, I pondered to myself, all you have to be is brave!

Annie Williams (11)
Heathcote School, Chingford

Some Hope And A Prayer

Every birthday, every Christmas, I prayed that you would come,
For eleven years, I still hoped, I stuck to my wish like a piece of gum,
I felt that my wish was just too much, my parents said I was being dumb.

Every birthday, I swear, the first thing on my list was always you!
Then on my birthday, I crossed my fingers, hoping that when I open my door I will see you,
But that morning never came, my heart sank like a stone in the sea.

From the days that the birds flew and when the sun shone,
To the days when the foxes huddled and the sun had gone,
I still prayed for your arrival.

Every Christmas, I swear, the first and only thing on my list was always you!
So on Christmas morning, I crossed my fingers, hoping that when I open my door you will appear.

Alicia Ramsamy (11)
Heathcote School, Chingford

I'm A Snowflake

They made fun of my nose, my lips, my eyes,
Kept telling me all these lies.
They told me I was loved,
But when I cried
No one was by my side.
So many times I wished I was like them
Until I realised I didn't need to.
I'm a person, a human,
I'm a powerful woman.
I am unstoppable,
I crushed every mould I was put in because I'm not mouldable.
I'm not a piece of clay to mould.
Instead, I'm an empty canvas to create my own world.
I don't care what others think,
'Cause I'm the only one who can paint.
My future, my destiny or me,
So I want to say something to those who judged me,
I'm not play dough,
I'm a snowflake
And I'm unique in my own way.

Ada Cinar (12)
Heathcote School, Chingford

Love Is Above

As long as the sun burns in the sky,
Then I will never have to say goodbye,
I will love you until the moon stops shining its light,
And when the clock strikes midnight,
Your imaginary knight will be waiting to fight,
He will propose and make your day bright,
And there he goes into the dark night.

I will love you till the day I die,
And hug you whenever you cry,
You gave me power, you gave me strength,
You listened to my problems of any lengths,
And for that, I just wanted to say thank you,
When I look into your deep blue eyes,
I have a burning feeling inside.

When you text me at night,
I feel like I'm gonna die.
As long as you and I cry,
We will always be alright.

Anna Klys (12)
Heathcote School, Chingford

Dear Future Self

May I ask you one small thing...
Am I mentally well?
Have I followed my road of dreams?
Am I afraid to derail from my dreams?
I just wanted to ask...

Are you happy?
Have you got people who make you love life?
Is the ride of life being fair?
I just wanted to ask...

I just wanted to tell you something...
Call your friends to go to the park,
Call your family, go to a restaurant,
Get your dog's lead and go make them enjoy life.
I just wanted to ask...

The last thing I wanted to say...
Stay healthy, go outside and have fun.
Life is short, be happy, a child can follow your footsteps
And create something new...

Ruben Tota (12)
Heathcote School, Chingford

My Football Life

Pass, shoot, score, football is my life,
Watching it, playing it, it was all fun and a good way to socialise
Until... the Euros 2020/2021, something terrible happened,
Rashford, Sancho and Saka missed a penalty in the final, never mind,
Some people minded,
Racist, racist, racist, some people said some horrible words, horrible names,
But I think the racist people are disgraceful people.
The three boys made a mistake, you should be grateful, all of them players got you to the final,
What would happen if we looked the same?
Same hair, same colour, same personality,
We are all different.
That is what I love about this wonderful world,
Come on, you Spurs.

Joel Murray (11)
Heathcote School, Chingford

This Is Reality

This is reality,
immortality is his legacy,
the people he inspired,
showed them reality.

Hearts beat and spines shiver,
but him,
he was bigger,
hs words were bigger.

This is reality,
as Dave said,
"The blacker the berry, the sweeter the juice,
but the blacker the killer, the sweeter the news."

But if you don't know
you're not meant to know,
just because you come from the ghetto,
doesn't mean you can't grow.

Yesterday is gone,
tomorrow is not promised,
today is a gift,
that's why it's called the present.

This
is
reality.

Emirhan Gultekin
Heathcote School, Chingford

Your Future Self

Have you ever thought of what you want to do when you are older?

Yes?

Well, let me ask...

How many times have you changed the job you have wanted?

I am going to guess you have, I think you have changed it more than once.

Have you ever stuck with the job you always wanted?

Well, I have.

I practised and practised doing the job that I wanted to do.

I got there in the end.

I have learnt what I need to do to get that job.

Even though I am eleven, I am trying hard to do my very best.

Now, if you haven't decided what you want to do when you are older,

It doesn't matter, all you have to do is follow your dreams.

Kayleigh Blain (11)
Heathcote School, Chingford

The Will Of Empowerment

Empowerment is a word that speaks courage,
Empowerment is a voice of strength,
It's what takes you beyond the place of yesterday
And towards the place of tomorrow.

We have faced the unexpected,
We have gone through challenges unaffected,
We fought the good fight,
That has led us to triumph.

Safe from judgement and fear,
Let us focus on encouraging our peers
And carry each other's buckets of tears,
To show that we care.

The journey has seemed long,
But let us keep marching on,
Because together we are strong.

Now that is true empowerment.

Destiny Sanusi (12)
Heathcote School, Chingford

Ode To Books

B efore books were ever made
O nce upon a time when people lived in a cave
O h, what on Earth did they used to do?
K illing time would be easier for me or you.

S adly, in times of old
T owns often went without books
O r lost a lot of gold
R ich people always had the books
Y ou and I have today to make us bold.

N ever read a book?
O h, how disgraceful!
V amp up your vocabulary with words like
'E cstatic' and 'graceful'
L oving books: the key to loving yourself.

Sophie Dolan (12)
Heathcote School, Chingford

Fight For Earth

E ndless amounts of plastic swims, thus

N arwals are endangered, due to us

V ast, lengthy summers corrode the land

I ce sheets are melting, we have to understand

R ain is becoming acidic, vegetables struggle to grow

O ases of land torn apart, nothing is aglow

N itrogen dioxide and CO2 pollute our air

M any people don't even care

E nlightened once but now pitch-black

N ight sky without stars, just an inky blanket

T he planet needs our help.

We have to fight with our Earth, not against it.

Amelia Bell (11)

Heathcote School, Chingford

Our Home

Our world is dying,
There isn't enough trying,
You have a choice,
Find your voice,
The icebergs have melted,
They can't be mended,
The pollution is suffocating,
Some find it hard breathing,
We aren't doing our best,
Is this some kind of test?
We have many famous scientists,
Not enough activists,
They have all these inventions,
We can save our home with good intentions,
So I ask you,
What are you doing to save your home?
So are you going to come?
This is not the world we had in mind,
So let's be more kind.

Tanimah Akther (12)
Heathcote School, Chingford

We Can All Be Different

We can all be different,
just like an apple, like the way that it has different seeds in
different places.
Even some areas of apples have different skin highlights.
Right? One apple can be bigger than the other one,
like snowflakes have different shapes and also different
types of sizes, even if we can't see them with our eyes.
What about planets?
We call them planets, but they all have different names,
colours, sounds, identities and looks...
Like Earth, has water and it's warm
but the sun is hotter, Uranus is cooler.
So what?
We can all be different.

Ruya Calili (11)
Heathcote School, Chingford

What You Have Done For Me

You gave me a life, you gave me a dream
You have given me hope in the future to become just like you
And that's why I chose you.

You have given me a future, you gave the power to me,
You have pushed me every day to become like you
And that's why I chose you.

You have never stopped me, you always kept on
And that's why I'm not alone...
Thanks to you.

You were and you are and you will be
The person who was and is and will be
The person who inspires me for my whole life.
Thank you for what you have done.

Sianna Dimitrova (12)
Heathcote School, Chingford

Underneath It All...

A place not known,
Where my hair isn't compared to the soft touch of a pillow,
So many times the only rest I get is after four.
Gossip running through the air thick and thin too,
"No one cares about Clarrisa," or, "Oh, she pulled up that finger."
Crying after school because of the 'banter'.
A different person hiding in a new persona.
Closed doors capture what is a wreck,
Only the strings under the surface realise the struggle,
Surface pressure is too much to hand.
But insecurity hits harder when you're... alone.

Kalifa Dennis (11)
Heathcote School, Chingford

Dear Past Me

Dear past me,
I know life is hard
but you have to just deal with it.

Dear past me,
I know you like him
but it's not worth it, trust me.

Dear past me,
it's now the future,
you have great friends
and life's not hard.

Dear past me,
you found someone new,
he's great and lovely,
he cares about you.

Dear past me,
just know that your life
gets better.

Dear past me,
yes, exams are hard
but you get through them,
don't worry, it will all be okay.

Josie Julie Knight (11)
Heathcote School, Chingford

Thank You, Jules

You are happy,
You are kind,
You are the brightest star in a universe full of life,
You are the reason I stopped crying,
Even when I felt like dying.

You gave me hope in my darkest hours
And told me that we could make the world ours,
You are like the sun spreading warmth and joy
To everyone around you.

You didn't give up on me when everyone else did,
You even helped me when I ran and hid,
If it wasn't for you then I wouldn't be the person that I am today,
So thank you, Jules, for all your love and care.

Lucy Holmes (12)
Heathcote School, Chingford

Motivation

M otivation is feeling that you can be who you want to be,

O pening a new chapter to discover a new person.

T he idea that you are powerful and strong.

I nvincible, capable of anything that comes your way, being

V ery joyful and positive.

A new beginning can start today because

T oday is a blessing.

I t can be the day you are at your happiest,

O r the day you feel your weakest.

N ot every day can be the best, but appreciate the good days, because those days mean the most.

Darcy Wilson (12)

Heathcote School, Chingford

Image

I am me
I'm not the girl with 130 million subscribers
I'm not the multibillionaire
I'm not no one.

I am me
I'm not a footballer with golden boots
I'm not a person with trophies
I'm not no one.

I am me
I'm not a famous person
I'm not a rich person
I'm not no one.

I am Loreta
I'm someone who tries
I'm someone who cries
I am someone.

I'm human
I'm me and that's something
You can't take away from me.

Loreta Fana (12)
Heathcote School, Chingford

Turn The Page

Everybody, everything
Is different.
Every story
Is different.
So many unique genres, so many, so many.
All the covers, so many, so different,
You don't judge them by their cover.
You get to know them -
Turn the page and start reading.
Turn the page, it's better than you thought,
Just keep reading, because you want to know.
A few more pages, keep going...
You finished, did you regret it or did you like it?
Were you glad you opened
The book you were too afraid to read?

Rosie Hutler (13)
Heathcote School, Chingford

Letter To My Future Self

Dear future me,
I will always aspire to be the best,
even when it rains I'll try to be better.

Even when the wind is howling I will blow back even harder
and when I'm in a room full of darkness
I will always find the light.

I will be the star that guides the boats.
I will be supportive, selfless and will never gloat.

No matter how tough life gets I will overcome it,
maybe not today, but tomorrow or another day
because I am a champion and I believe in myself.

Jack Avanzi (11)
Heathcote School, Chingford

Trapped

Is there something trapped in your mind?
Something that you can't get rid of,
Something that you're too shy or not confident to talk
about.
Well, try something new and tell your friends or family
So that it can get out of your head.
Don't be shy,
Don't be non-confident,
Don't be a butterfly and fly away from your problems,
Be a bee flying towards pollen like flying to your problems,
Confidence is what you need
And a key for the next generation to see.

Tayla Walton (12)
Heathcote School, Chingford

Equality And Racial Discrimination

This world is full of toxic discrimination,
it's hard to believe that this is our nation,
the racial slurs,
the hurtful words,
but at the end of the day, this is our world.

Day by day racism is being thrown,
even by those who are old or grown,
it's a normality to society and happens all over the world,
respect for every race or ethnicity is all so curled,
our world is toxic and needs to be fixed,
but the racial discrimination in it makes me sick.

Desharna Bailey-Hanley (12)
Heathcote School, Chingford

Destiny

Life is a journey
and you are the driver
you've just gotta put in the work
and put in the hours.

You've gotta stay hungry
and you will devour
you've gotta try the hardest
and work the smartest

because you are you
and you have the power
to know what's right
and to strive to be better each hour.

You have to put in the work
and put in the hours
and when the time is right
we'll take what's ours.

Farhan Mahmood (12)
Heathcote School, Chingford

Everyone

Everyone should live life to the fullest,
Not sitting around in school, thinking you're the coolest.

Everyone has a passion, everyone has a goal,
Don't waste it or throw it down a hole.
Everyone wants to do something,
For example, playing the acoustic.
That's why our hearts have beats, just like music.

Everyone should help someone,
Like the homeless as they have nothing to devour,
That's why we have the company empowered.

Josh Terumalai (13)
Heathcote School, Chingford

Be Yourself

Beneath the surface we are all the same
There is no race or gender
No need to call people names
But individuality makes you unique and one of a kind
So don't be afraid to share what's on your mind.

Bring out your values and don't be shy
Respect who you are
And as time goes by
Your dignity will arise.

All the challenges that you go through
Will make you stronger
And you will do
What you need to pull through.

Jessica Lupu (13)
Heathcote School, Chingford

Not The Perfect You

I'm not perfect, I'm never perfect
Perfection is the light I can't reach
The negative I must disinfect
I will push myself to the end

I will struggle
I will be pressured
But I will never stop
Until I reach the top

Of the mountain
I will fall
I will fail
But I will never be derailed

I will not fit in
I will not be the same as everyone else
But I am not perfect
I'm not perfect.

Yuhua Wang (12)
Heathcote School, Chingford

Act, Don't Think

Help others
like they are your sisters and brothers.
Do your best
and forget about the rest.
Forget about the winning or the losing,
just have fun without the bruising.
You are as special
as all the other people.
You are who you want to be,
just set yourself free.
Put in the work
and take what you deserve.
You change your game,
so remember your pride and your name.
Now you need to empower everyone you see.

Dylan Aslan (13)
Heathcote School, Chingford

My Bouncy Ambition

On the court
Sweating, going for the ball,
I need to be careful or I'll fall.

Trying to get to my ambition,
I've got loads of missions,
I need to be careful or I'll fall.

Obstacles trying to break me or shatter me,
Avoiding them with no concern, empowering myself,
I need to be careful or I'll fall.

I have reached the top,
I have not got mopped,
I have achieved what I was meant to be.

Emir Boztepe (11)
Heathcote School, Chingford

Planet Of Diversity

Identity is the more of me
We do our best when we become we.
Some days we lose ourselves
While others move themselves.
The length you've gone through
Shows the strength you've gained too
But who am I?
When it's right,
There's light.
We're unequal but equal.
While some live in comfortability,
Others live in vulnerability
But we have the ability to make unity
On the Planet of Diversity.

Vanesa Lwanga (13)
Heathcote School, Chingford

Unobtainable Perfection

Odd one out, unwanted attention.
I want to reach, reach out for perfection.
In a city of women, I'm a useless reflection.
Unable to be one of them.
I'm just a shadow, a shadow of excellence.
I want to fit in, I want to breathe with them.
I want, I want perfection.
I am a dead daisy in a field of lively roses.
Eventually, I'll grow.
The seeds will flourish.
But I still want the unobtainable perfection.

Aisha Cogliandro (13)
Heathcote School, Chingford

Wondering

I am me,
I may not be as tall as the trees,
But that won't stop me making me, me.
Maybe being me might mean I will swim to victory,
Maybe being me might mean I will run till the tape breaks
into pieces,
Maybe just maybe it's in my genes,
The competitive and powerful girl I am might have come
from my mother.
The brave and confident girl I am might have come from my
father
And that's just sort of my identity.

Ava Allison (11)
Heathcote School, Chingford

Too Much

Help.
This is too much for my young mind to cope.
This is too much - I'm losing all my hope.
This is too much - I'm losing my mind.
This is too much - I've lost myself and can't find...
Find my way out of this maze.
They all tell me, "This is just a phase."
I can't take it anymore.
What was all of this for?
I'm going to speak out, there's too much on my mind.
There is the exit I longed to find.

Ashirah Defroand (13)
Heathcote School, Chingford

Women's Rights

Every woman has the right to speak.
Some people might think that we're weak,
but that's all they see.
Some people think that women
are only here to cook and clean,
I'm not trying to make a scene
but that's quite mean.
Women have dreams too,
like we all do.
So please treat women with respect
and forget the phrase,
'Women belong in the kitchen'
because it's incorrect.

Maryam Asid (12)
Heathcote School, Chingford

Rising Up

Raised.
One fist changed into millions,
Maybe one day it'll be billions.
How can so many things become just a list?

They're fed up and done,
With the discrimination.
An overpowered government against a nation.

Giving the nights they never had before.
Before this chance ever happened,
They were scared and confused about what will come.

Now is their time to rise up.

Talia Edwards (12)
Heathcote School, Chingford

You Helped Me

You gave me hope, you gave me luck,
You helped me when I was stuck.
You trusted me when I was untrustable
And for that I'm thankful.
You wiped my tears when I was sad,
Helped me to get ready.
You are my world and my hero,
You will always be here for me
Through hard and good times
And when you're gone, I will be sad
So sad I'll be mad.

April Foley (12)
Heathcote School, Chingford

Equal Rights

Everyone should be treated equally
No one should be treated unevenly
Everyone should be the same
No one has any shame.

No one should be neglected for the colour of their skin
Or the way that they think
Everyone should be united
And forever feel invited

Everyone has a chance to be free
Everyone should be able to be.

Buse Boran (13)
Heathcote School, Chingford

The Past

The past was good
but the present is better.
Never say never,
as the future's gonna get you.

There's always time to change
but it's in your range.
A lot of stuff is new,
but just be you.

Here's the future
and say bye to the past.
As the future hits fast,
just remember now is a blast.

Ashton Alvarez (12)
Heathcote School, Chingford

Calm Cat

Dear cat,
Every time I feel a bit stressed,
I don't feel sad
Because you take it out,
When I'm out and about,
When I'm a bit foxed,
You make me feel relaxed,
Because I stroke your fur
And then you purr.
Every time I eat my food,
You start eating too.
You act like a human
And I look after you.

Ayla Candaner (11)
Heathcote School, Chingford

Potential

Waiting for a chance,
The time to prove,
The time to act,
But if only I could,
The strength, the courage,
The thing I lack,
But the thing I want.
I must continue,
I must prevail,
Think out of the box,
Break out of my cage,
Break out of yours,
The time is now,
Take the chance,
When it counts.

Ilir Gashi (12)
Heathcote School, Chingford

The Loud Silence

I try to breathe and gasp for air.
My voice is here, for the people who care.
I want to speak, I want to shout
But to my surprise, not a sound comes out.
I'm aching to speak, without a doubt.
I scream and shout,
The words come out.

But no one listened, no one cared.
I try to breathe,
To gasp for air.

Paige Stein (12)
Heathcote School, Chingford

Family

F ood finished with a touch of love

A lways ready to make me laugh

M aking fun days out to find hearts in harmony

I nner spirits break free to create magical memories

L ove is always near when you're with family

Y oung and old hearts fuse together to make never-ending laughter.

Mairah Asghar (11)

Heathcote School, Chingford

Women's Rights

Women's rights should be accepted,
not neglected.

Women should be encouraged
and supported, not discouraged.

Women should be allowed to make their decisions,
not go by people's opinions.

Women are strong, powerful and brave,
women's rights should be embraced.

Kezia Amedume (13)
Heathcote School, Chingford

Sport Is Unique

Football, basketball, tennis
the different sports you do make you unique
even if you're having fun
or going for a run.

It makes you unique,
the games you play,
how you go your way.

It makes you unique,
everything makes you unique,
in every way possible.

Ryan Thomson (12)
Heathcote School, Chingford

The Lone Moon

I'm lonely and sad
as I'm the moon.
A lone fighter
watching the stars get together.

I'm lonely and sad
as I'm the moon
until I realise
the people looking up at me, through their windows

are lonely and sad too.

Rosie Keuning (12)
Heathcote School, Chingford

If Misogyny Didn't Exist

Why is it when it comes to women,
we are treated differently?
When we get the same job as a man,
why is our salary lower?
Why are we expected to be as sweet as a flower?
And we're expected to be perfect for men,
every second, every hour.

Sofia Halacheva (12)
Heathcote School, Chingford

To My Future Self

To my future self, make sure to check on the ones you love.
To my future self, if you have a dream, try as hard as you
can to succeed.
To my future self, keep a smile.
To my future self, make sure to keep good friends.
To my future self, enjoy life.

Mason Steck (12)
Heathcote School, Chingford

Heavy Water

They cling to me like heavy water,
Ever dragging me down,
I want to escape, I must, without them finding out,
They will not let me go,
They pull me into a darkness unlike all others,
They say, "Do we not care for you?
Do we not love you?"
But these demons feed on my tears.
I cannot escape,
They cling to me like heavy water,
They will not let go as they drag me down towards a darkness unlike all others,
I must escape yet I cannot,
There is no escape, no end to this torment.
I hear their voices, beckoning,
I must stay away...
It is impossible, it is subtle, it is folly...
They cling to me like heavy water,
There is no escape,
They cling to me like heavy water,
"Do we not love you?"
The voices are distorted, dripping with malice.
I cannot escape, but I must,
I must escape...
I can escape and I will as the voices become dulled,
I can escape and I will, I can escape and I will.

Nafsica Ladas (15)

Hyndland Secondary School, Hyndland

The Suffragettes

Struggling from the start,
the women of the world grow brighter
prejudice sets them apart.
They are called Freedom Fighters.

As they shout from the rooftops,
they use their freedom of speech as their power, their
rampage had few stops.
Their message bloomed like a flower.

Conquering the world
place by place,
running through countries as their skirts twirled, they put a
name to their face.

They published their aim in the Gazette.
They left the men around them upset.
These more than 50,000 women were seen as the threat.
Women across the world send thanks and will never forget,

who they were or what they stood for,
they were called the Suffragettes.

Darbie Veness (17)
Mulberry UTC, Bow

What We Need

Pain rises from strength like yeast in a Victoria sponge
The strength to prolong all the shame
Knowing you've lost
The strength to smile when all you feel is anger
To substitute bad days for the best ones you can remember
The strength to say, "I'm lost," when your pride is blocked
To say, "Please love me," though I've never done it right

When you learned to love yourself
You began to feel everything come alive around me
Sunflowers bursting at the seams
As your release opened the door to new beginnings
Where I found strength and power.

Frankie Hudson-Green
Ormiston Beachcroft Academy, London

Power

Power smells like charcoal.
Power smells like the predator and its prey.
Power is the taste of steak.
Power pollutes people's minds and makes them think they're a higher power than those around them.
Power strikes fear into people's hearts like a lion's roar!
If I had power, I would make the world a better place by making people care, stop pollution and the destroying of earth.
Power's like lions leaping into battle...
Steak smells strong
And powerful... predators prey on weaker animals.

Oren Gerald-Williams (11)
Ormiston Beachcroft Academy, London

The Earth

The Earth is a vehicle driving
us around the sun

too much intelligence
too much power against animals

we messed up the world for future generations
Earth is orbiting

Earth breathes for us
movement magnet walking

our planet is a blue beauty
and a beautiful seed.

Ali Rida (11)
Ormiston Beachcroft Academy, London

Puff

Always questioning myself twenty-four.
I've no idea, my mind goes blank.
Wait, will I be powerful?
Will I fulfil my dreams?
Tell me now!
It's all just a blur,
Clouds... clouds
Just go
Puff!

Rezan Muhammed (16)
Ormiston Beachcroft Academy, London

How To Win In Life

Be humble towards your surroundings.
Don't be the light bulb in the room,
You say, "You can't see the path."
Can you see your next steps?
Cautiously.
Be more
Great!

Tariq Noor
Ormiston Beachcroft Academy, London

Magic

Something I do when I'm bored - magic.
Sitting alone at home - magic.
Abracadabra magic.
Dreams we have are magic.
Imagine magic.
We are magic.
Magic is very real.

Seysha
Ormiston Beachcroft Academy, London

A Million Faces

I'm wise but dumb. I'm happy and sad.
I can be convincing but mad.
How did I end up here?
I am misled
Sometimes.
One million
Disguises.
Unwise,
Yes.

Masood Ridha
Ormiston Beachcroft Academy, London

Martyrs Don't Die

We do not fear,
For a fool will learn nothing from wise people,
But wise people will learn much from fools,
You do this in the name of our religion,
We do it, not to break humanity's jewels.

They left you with a life,
They could've ended you all right.
One single knife,
A never-ending light.

121 angels,
121 deaths,
121 mothers,
Beating their chests.

Roj Almohammad (14)

Parrs Wood High School, East Didsbury

I Remember A Time...

I remember a time when I was a little girl,
I was playing in a play centre with my new pal.
I was crawling through tunnels, climbing up walls until some
little kid couldn't ignore the fact that I was black.
I had dark skin, he looked at me and thought I belonged in a
bin.
He called me a brownie, my heart then split, *crack!*
I ran to my mother, I didn't have anybody other.
I cried in her arms, begging for help,
She told me not to listen, to continue playing by myself.
I looked her in the eyes, I couldn't believe that my mum had
told me to just let it be.
I felt alone, it stung like a bee.
The feeling hurt, it was quite bittersweet.
As a young black child, I found this alarming.
That my own mother dearest wouldn't be my Prince
Charming.
You're black, you're black,
You're darker than the rest.
That was the voice that kept booming in my head.
Now that I've grown, I look back on the situation.
After all that's gone on, I have hope for this generation.
George Floyd, Breonna Taylor, Ahmaud Arbery and others,
Grandmothers, sisters, mothers and brothers
Crying for the life of the relative that was taken.
If you were put in this position would you not be shaken?

Black girls and boys scared to leave 'cause the white people
fear that the blacks might thieve.
If we look much deeper when will we see that no matter the
colour we all still bleed?
This little piece was for all the blacks,
I wanted you to know that no matter what they say
The love for you is as clear as the day.
You should embrace your skin no matter the colour,
It doesn't matter what you look like,
We are all human.
After all the abuse we receive do they think we're
superhuman?
You can be what you want to be no matter what they think.
If you want to write with ink,
Dance or go to an ice rink or even mix drinks
Who are they to judge?
If we can spread the word, we can raise awareness
To make sure everybody is treated with fairness.
If we put our heads together we can blossom like flowers.
My name's Aminah and I'm here to empower.

Aminah Ajala-Edwards (14)
Parrs Wood High School, East Didsbury

Heartbroken Kid

Yeah, I know I put you through pain
and have been told I was going to change.
You gave me chance after chance
but the issue continues the same.
You left me, now you're all about money,
I'm so happy you wanna get paid,
I loved and it's sad you don't love me,
it's my fault, so you I can't blame.
I try and show I'm different,
it's kinda true, all guys are the same,
had dreams of you, enough visions,
but all the time we spent was a waste,
late nights in my room, I'm lonely.
It's kinda hurting watching us fade,
I'm trying to let go and let you move on
but it hurts to see you away from me,
baby girl, you are my rock,
I thought we were meant to be,
guess not 'cause you're not with me,
it's 5am and I still can't sleep,
reminiscing good times we had,
kinda wish it was all a dream,
kinda wish you never noticed me,
but you did, now my soul just bleeds.

Look, I messed up all my blessings,
never learnt from my lessons,
stressed in my room, popping anti-depressants,
you loved me in the past, now you don't in the present,
spoke about you to my Marje, now I wish I didn't.

Abubakar Bhatti (13)
Parrs Wood High School, East Didsbury

Youth

Kids nowadays, always on social media,
Unnecessary information, like an encyclopedia.
Getting influenced to become a thug on the road,
Dying just because of their postcode.

Mothers burying their children, it's just not right,
All this darkness, what happened to the light?
Animosity, hostility, negativity,
What happened to the smiles and the happy energy?

Bullying and social exclusion,
Thug life is just a delusion.
Selling drugs just to make figures,
They leave out the part where you have to pull triggers.

Take someone's life,
Take someone's wife,
Carry a knife,
Or maintain a strife.

Why be a molester
And frightened the streets of Manchester?
Please pick education
Over probation.
Don't cause frustration,
But make unity in your nation.

All this violent fighting,
Criminal cases multiplying,
And these bars that I'm reciting,
In this poor handwriting,
Is for you to do your parents proud,
Or stand in front of a crowd
And exclaim out loud,
That you made the right decision,
Had the correct vision
And everyone watching you
On television.

Abbas Kazemi (12)
Parrs Wood High School, East Didsbury

Never Undo

I waited for you,
I waited for you

I made a mistake
I can never undo

and now I look back
but then I lost track

it hurt so bad
I can never go back

I could wait forever
but then I won't learn

that memories fade
no matter how much it hurts

and on the inside
I feel my heart cry

I'm tearing at the walls
in the corner of my mind

I waited for you
I waited for you

I made a mistake
I can never undo

I still remember
the tangle we were

but in the end
what did we give it up for?

It was so small
worth nothing at all

but it was my everything
and now it's lost.

Bilal Hussain (13)
Parrs Wood High School, East Didsbury

Live For Our Own Freedom

Everyone has their own right,
We all need to speak, think, learn, write.
Speak out our own words,
Think about how to build a better world,
Learn how to be a better youth,
Write out to spread the truth.
Everyone deserves these rights,
But some might feel contrite.
Everyone lives for freedom,
No one can ever break the system.

Cheuk Tung Lui (13)
Parrs Wood High School, East Didsbury

Our Planet

Why is it so hard *not* to throw plastic away?

There's no need for it
But people say we don't want it to stay.

Everything is not okay
It's slowly killing the planet in front of our eyes
The oceans and seas aren't alright.

It's just strangling the world and everything here
We pray that this world will continue as a sphere.
So now I say again *don't* throw the plastic away.

So let's stop pollution today, okay?
Even if it's just you and me, we can spread the word
It doesn't need to be all the herd,
Why can people not see climate change is real and true,
It doesn't need to be a message that's all blue.
I can't be silenced anymore, I need to be heard
'Cause animals are precious and I'm spreading the word
So once more I say *don't* throw the plastic away

Let's get this movement in motion today.

Sophia Alexander (12)
Ratcliffe College, Ratcliffe On The Wreake

Inside A Girl's Brain

Mumma always said, "If you ever seem a stranger following you, you go to the other side of the street."
And that's something we had to learn at a young age because we're just young fiends.
If you ever show too much body,
you would get the boys looking at you from head to toe,
them all thinking I am a doll,
they also need to check if I'm pretty,
otherwise, I'd be an embarrassment and make them look silly.
Is it a new rule or am I just a tool?
This society has made me scared to walk in public,
wondering who is the next person to look at me in a weird way.
They don't care about I have to say,
it's always about what they want and what they think,
never about what I want or how I'm feeling nowadays.

Tania Begum (13)
Regent High School, Camden

Kievan Spring

Once, when Kiev was in spring, everything felt alive.
Those were truly the best moments in my life, free, lively and joyous
Dashing, diving, drifting and skiving, my days were truly wondrous
Oh, how I wistfully long for this sanguine feeling to come back.

These memories are now trapped in a mist of sombre anguish
And although far apart from my current life, remember these like yesterday.
Now Kiev is experiencing a spring, long gone were the screams of children in the park and the rubber soles of children's shoes
Replaced by screams of protestors and the rubber bullets fired swiftly by policemen, conflict budding from under the gravel
My once full and crowded drive was a bleak and vandalised slum.

Now my soul and spirit dead, I often ponder and replay spring in my head
I want to scream and cry for aid and for this all to stop
But I am just a small fish in a colossal ocean, as powerful as a feather falling to the ground.
Once, in Kiev, there was spring, freedom and new ideas shone through, that was a long time ago.

Isaac Noblett (13)
Rockport School, Craigavad

My Poem

Year 8, started messing around at school,
standing up to people, the confidence it gave me felt like fuel,
now I'm just realising how it was cruel,
fitting in with people, making new friends,
having to apologise to teachers, trying to make amends.
My mental health was low,
I knew I could do something to help myself,
but I was just too slow and so I got sucked into a whirlpool.
Everyone was telling me I was wasting school,
but I preferred being seen as cool.
I used to be a girl whose life was on track,
but slowly everything faded to black.
Depression, anxiety, it was an attack,
I cared about surviving,
not as much about getting back on track.
It feels like I'm screaming but no one can hear,
no one knows how severe and I blame that down to fear.
School said, "There are rules here, you must adhere,"
but the stress was so overwhelming, like a voice in my ear,
the way I was headed I had no chance at a career,
I just wanted to disappear.
I started seeing a therapist,
recovery seems like climbing all the way up Mount Everest,
but bit by bit, step by step, I will get there,
to the point where I care, and I am aware.

This feeling and true happiness can't even compare,
I will no longer be in despair,
I will feel as though I can finally repair.
So anyone who's struggling out there,
do what you can to help yourself,
so you can put this chapter of your life back on the shelf.
Do it before you get sucked into the whirlpool like me,
I guarantee there is someone out there to help you find the key and you can be set free.

Olivia Andrews (13)
Sir Robert Pattinson Academy, North Hykeham

Life

Life is like a game of tag,
sometimes you're chasing interviews or friendships,
other times you might be the one being chased
for those things or something different
but the most important thing to remember is
whenever you trip or get pushed, always get back up again,
if you don't get that job, keep looking,
if you don't get that friendship, pick yourself up,
try to find a new friend.
Most importantly, embrace whatever life throws your way,
being fired, a medical condition,
because the longer it takes to get up in the game of tag,
the further your goals will get.

William Kearns (12)
Sir Robert Pattinson Academy, North Hykeham

People Of The Street

Stand around and wait for news.
Everyone aching with the flu.
You're sat at home, having a feast,
We're out here, looking and living like beasts.
"Help! Help! My child is dead!"
Apparently, we're not right in the head.
We are the poor! We live on the streets!
Don't be surprised if you see us begging at your feet.
We just need food! Even a crust of bread.
What's the point of living when we're dead?
We are the poor! The people of the streets.
We would give our left arm just to eat.

Phoebe Wilson (11)
Sir Robert Pattinson Academy, North Hykeham

If I Could Do Anything

If I could do anything I would climb the highest mountains
If I could do anything I would sway with the trees
If I could do anything I would fly with the birds
If I could do anything I would be blown away by the winter breeze
If I could do anything I would ride polar bears
If I could do anything I would swim with the fish
If I could do anything I would dance with the flowers
If I could do anything I would go to the moon
If I could do anything I would.

Ellie Dalton (12)
Sir Robert Pattinson Academy, North Hykeham

The Rain On Their Windows

The rain would tap on her window
As she felt like she was drowning in her own sorrow,
For she felt so alone,
Whilst she sat by the window inside her home.

The rain would tap on her window,
As the tears fell to his pillow,
For he felt so alone,
Whilst he sat on his bed inside his home.

The rain would tap on their windows,
Two different situations happening at once,
Yet they weren't so different
And neither alone.

Taya Garrard (13)
Sir Robert Pattinson Academy, North Hykeham

Empowered

I am a bee
so small no one can see.
Pretty some say
but only once a day.
Like a fish I swim and swim
only to lose a limb.
Prom queen on repeat
I don't even eat.
The world doesn't stop for me,
I wish I could be that bee.
I feel all alone,
I am just skin and bone.
"Eat a burger," they say.
I just want this feeling to go away.
How am I meant to feel empowered
when I am a coward?

Molly Waker (12)
Sir Robert Pattinson Academy, North Hykeham

A Random Bald Person (Leo)

I know it can be a bit wild,
Hold on, I hear a screaming child.
But no need to fear,
For this random bloke is here.

He will save the day,
We will all shout hooray.
Forget his mistakes,
Like that time at the lake.

He will get this child,
Back into the wild.
The child will be free,
As soon you will see,
From zero to hero, his name, Leo.

Aiden Nixon (14)
Sir Robert Pattinson Academy, North Hykeham

The Power Of Sports

S ports help to clear the mind
P laying them makes you forget about the time
O ver and over until you perfect the trick
R esilience is the key to nailing it
T ogether as one, you all thrive
S ports help to clear the mind.

Daisy Shrimpton (13)
Sir Robert Pattinson Academy, North Hykeham

The Wind Of Youth

The wind of youth blows
Helping the will of fire grow
'Cause if it ever leaves the leaf
We'd have no place to go
To fight for what we love
To defend what we hold dear
This isn't about our pride
Or about gods up above
Our own desires pushed aside
Fighting out of fear
For our friendships
For all that's good
To defend those things so pure
We should all do what we should
We should stand up against evil
We can be the cure
Our dreams won't be shattered.

Antonio Morgan-McGhie (12)
Southfields Academy, Wandsworth

Do You Know How Much You're Loved?

Let me be your dictionary,
Defining all your words.
Let me be your eggs,
Hatching all your birds.
Let me be your sunglasses
Protecting your eyes from the sun.
Let me be yours.

Let me be your screwdriver,
Securing all your screws,
But also be your wrench,
Making those screws loose.
Let me be your shoemaker,
Keeping intact your sole.
Just let me be yours.

Let me be your pen,
Writing all your notes.
Let me be your sailor,
Rowing all your boats.
Let me be your castle walls
Surrounded by a moat
Higher than the highest heaven
And deeper than any root

Just let me be
Just let me be...
Yours!

Codi Weston (13)
Southfields Academy, Wandsworth

Mirror Image

I sit by the mirror
the broken pieces lie by me

I did it again
I let them in my head

mirror in hand
why can't they just let me be?
They're in my head
even in my bed

why can't they just let me be me?

Ten years later
I straighten my hair
they've finally gone
the words they had said
the mirror that was once
broken is now mended.

Scarlett Spencer (13)
Southfields Academy, Wandsworth

I Wanna Be A Football Player

I wanna be a footballer
Football means happiness to me in many ways
Playing football could even earn me lots of money
Hard work and motivation will only help me get money from playing football
Hopefully, I will become a footballer
I will teach my brother how to become one as well.

Denzel Opoku Aboagye (12)
Southfields Academy, Wandsworth

Football

"Goal! Goal! Goal!" say the crowd
Your manager is very proud
When you do your skills
People know you pay the bills
The crowd finishes all the fun
Once our team have won
At night I rainbow flick
Then I remember my dad, Rick
Who lives with my uncle Nick.

Danny Boreham (12)
Southfields Academy, Wandsworth

School Can Suck

School might help
But does it help us mentally?
No, there are many reasons why
First, you make us burnt out
Second, you give us that pressure
Third, we get in trouble for talking
Four, you give us rules that you break
Five, school can suck!

Sidra Tul Muntha Shaikh (12)
Southfields Academy, Wandsworth

Football

Football is the little sun that guides me all the way
Football is my chosen path that will help me along the way
Football is the magic game that makes me feel so free
Football is my everything
That's why I love it so dearly.

Christian Cummings (12)
Southfields Academy, Wandsworth

When I Grow Up

When I grow up
I will explore science
Search until I can't
When I grow up
I will reach physics
Gravity will pull me to success
When I grow up
I will reach the limit of space
The limit that never ends.

Rodrigo Carvalho (12)
Southfields Academy, Wandsworth

Life Itself

A flower's colours look as bright as daylight
As it shines throughout the day
Sunlight symbolises happiness in the world
The sky shows wondrous colours from time to time
But can show sadness too...

Krystal Donaldson (13)
Southfields Academy, Wandsworth

Pizza

Munch, munch, munch your pizza
Eat while it is hot
Melted cheese and pepperoni
I sure want a lot
Ham, olives, green peppers
Canadian bacon too
Pineapple and sauce
You can make it too!

Danni Leite (13)
Southfields Academy, Wandsworth

Her Love, Her Life

She told me about the stars, galaxies and constellations,
Like Orion's Belt and the Lucky Dipper,
And she made me keep a lookout on the night sky
Whenever I had the chance to.

I asked her my questions
She gave me answers that even Google couldn't provide.
I gave her my time,
She gave me her pride
And she told me, "Don't be too arrogant,
But don't stop believing in yourself
And always be kind."

She told me about art
And how it's not meant to be 'pretty' or 'perfect' per se,
It's meant to be unique and expressive
Because it's yours at the end of the day!

She showed me her passions,
I showed her my work,
Which conveyed everything we'd dreamed of
And everything we'd talked about,
She was my best supporter and toughest critic,
Without a shadow of doubt.

She told me to go out and chase my dreams
And not to be guided by fear,
But by hope
And I was willing to go the distance; far or near.

She taught me to dance like no one's watching,
To sing and shout in the rain,
To live life on my own terms,
So that no one could rain on my parade.

But best of all...
She taught me not to put myself down, but to draw stars
around my scars,
For we're all beautiful just the way we are,
All love, no hate,
We're all human, we're all unbelievably great!

She is in you
And she is in me
And although she is gone,
Her gracious legacy still lives on,
In the lives of all of us, and all we can be.

Alexia Malaluan (14)
St Anne's Catholic High School For Girls, Enfield

The Library

Her mind was a library
Filled with the stories of beautiful lives, beautiful people
Maybe you'd have just a sentence, or a page, or a chapter
or two
Maybe you'd be the main event, a whole series, whole
shelves solely dedicated to you.

Maybe you'd be in a book that she'd never touch,
Maybe you're in one she won't dare put down,
Maybe you're in that one book tucked away in a corner
titled 'I Love You'
She'd never dare open it, even if her life depended on it
Because she loves you
Because she thinks that you're an angel
So don't hold back your wings.

She wrote them all with the ink of her past
The pages made of love
Bound together with her soul
And even if she's hidden you and you're all tucked away
She loves you
And she's written about you with the ink of her love.

And just imagine, of all the stories she's penned
You're in one of them

And even if society won't flick just one page
She will, I will
Because she loves you
I love you.

Amelia Malaluan (14)
St Anne's Catholic High School For Girls, Enfield

Just Two Weeks?

Tell us it's okay, tell us there's nothing to worry about.
Tell us it's just a two-week break.
Suddenly, 1,000 cases. *Tick... tick.* "Wear your mask."
10,000 cases. *Tick... tick.* "Social distance."
15,000 cases. *Tick... tick.* "Isolate."
35,000 cases. *Tick... tick.* "Stay home."
1,000,000 cases. *Tick... tick... tick...*
1,000,000... *boom!*

It never was okay from the start,
We went to go stay in our homes for a year.
"Thank you, NHS."
Children everywhere learning from home,
Adults working from home.
"Thank you, NHS."
Late nights, late mornings.
Is it Thursday or Tuesday?
I've got that work I need to complete.
"Thank you, NHS."
We know now that it's not okay.
We know we need to worry.
Because there is much longer than two weeks still to come our way.

Wanda Siwiec (11)
St Anne's Catholic High School For Girls, Enfield

Oh, You'll Be Fine

Oh, you'll be fine,
you don't really have anxiety,
you just stare at that phone all day,
you're not getting therapy.

Oh, you'll be fine,
just go to sleep early,
you're not an insomniac,
then in the morning you won't be surly.

Oh, you'll be fine,
if you want a solution,
to you being depressed
ignore it, that'll be a revolution.

Oh, you'll be fine,
you don't have OCD,
you're just attention-seeking,
you need to sort out your priorities.

Oh, you'll be fine,
bipolar isn't what you are,
you're just going through puberty,
you're not broken with scars.

Don't just say, "Oh, you'll be fine,"
you are not in their position,
just be kind
and make them feel relaxed.

Humayrah Salamuthally (11)
St Anne's Catholic High School For Girls, Enfield

Hush

The subtlety of silence, yet everything was known.
Despite the bounds and barriers, the bravery was shown.
Through the mists of the pain, and taboo of the past.
Through the people and the places that kept us apart.
There's been a disparity between our thoughts,
Unseen efforts to cut through these knots.
Tangled among two separate ends,
Silence echoed in utter shame.

Keyuri Ade (16)
St Leonards School, St Andrews

The Trailing Steps Of Those That Left

"But I have no sense of self," I joke.
He smiles, "Then write about that."
But how? How do I write about something,
When that something is so foreign to me?

When I think of my friends
I see colours, shades of pink, blue and purple.
I hear songs, notes ringing on the wind.
They are familiar.

When I think of my family
I see waves crashing along a boat by the sea.
I hear shouts, screaming and shattering glass.
They are my home.

When I think of my past.
I know little of where I stood, and where I've been.
But I see a box in the ground, my mother weeping.
I hear the beep of a monitor as I lie chained
Locked in a room of pasty white, flocks of masked monsters
waving by.
I try to forget.

So maybe they are that sense of self.
My past, my family, my friends.

They are what makes me... me.
It's a nice thought.

"I don't know how to write." I frown.
And as I step out, back into the crowd, his smile fades.
I didn't catch what he said as I walked off.
Just write something.

When I think of myself
I see, and I hear, but I don't know.
I walk this Earth with everyone else, and yet
No matter where I am, I'm lost.

When you think of me,
I wonder, do you smile fondly?
Or do you shake your head and walk on?
Have you moved on?

"But I have no sense of self," I repeat.
And I hear him again, "Then write about that."
But how do I write about something
Of which the very concept frightens me?

So that's what I'll do.
I'll trudge up memories, in the name of art
Rob the dead of their right to rest.
So I can write.

Alex O'Reilly (16)
St Mark's High School, Warrenpoint

Pink Forearms Of A She-Mantis

The clock clicks... day by day,
As she goes astray,
She's caught by the tail once again.

Now she's tugging and pulling me closer,
I am aware this time it's too late,
As I don't have enough courage to muster,
She's caught me once again.

She dug her into my chest,
As her bright pink forearms are covered in red,
I struggle to breathe, to talk, to call out!
Will I ever be free again?

It feels like forever since she's caught me,
I'm not the one to blame,
Her words are sweet and fun to play with,
I feel myself slip away.

It's too comfortable, too warm,
Too fluffy, I feel unsafe,
My blood arises, my fury surges,
I will take my last final breath.

I'll kick, I'll pull, I'll itch for glory,
I'll rip and tear from these hooks,
Until I can taste bittersweet victory!

My feelings are frail,
As my plan starts to fail,
Her grip tightens into an uncomfortable rage,

But I misjudged my failure,
My tears are real, my one final tug,
The mantis pops out her elbows, bellowing with fear.

I finally push, and set myself free,
Running, and gasping for air,
With the widest of smiles, my chest is free,
As I taste guilty victory.

The things I've missed, I look forward to,
And I'm learning to love myself again,
As these wounds heal into scars
I'm starting to see the beauty in them.

I get lost in myself.
I've forgotten her face, her voice, her words,
I'm growing, learning and yearning to fix my scars.

She can never catch me ever again.

Lena Cendrowska (16)
St Mark's High School, Warrenpoint

A Soldier's Armour

Like a soldier preparing for battle, I am preparing for war
I put armour around my heart, hopefully sparing me from
bullets
Then grab my ammunition, the only self-defence I have
against my nemesis
I then steel my nerves, my heart, my mind and creep in like a
serpent

Automatically, I am hit with the bullets of hate comments on
my recent social media post: 'If I were a lame loser like you,
I'd end myself'
A tsunami is all I see, all I feel, all the sadness builds and
builds until it erupts, like Mount Vesuvius,
The armour which I have worked so hard melding has
shattered and I am left vulnerable for attack.
The empowerment of social media is a tear gas that blinds
its victims.
I scatter to try and melt my armour back together in
desperation... as I scroll down some more.
I am blinded by the light of a comment, 'you are beautiful,
don't let anyone tell you the opposite'.

Now, I am here today, my armour like Excalibur;
And I am here to strengthen you, for a soldier's armour is as
tough as steel, but ours will be even stronger.

Rhianna McKenna (16)
St Mark's High School, Warrenpoint

Unconditional Self-Love

Your own self deserves the love you crave
So why treat yourself as a slave?
Standards in this society do not control you
You deserve to live your life as a soul living free,
I do what is best for me without fearing the unknown
I express self-love to thrive without persevering,
I disclose myself with no back doors
While showing empowering and emphasising my roars.

Being me is hard sometimes
Left with a despondency of walls to climb,
But once I hit my mark
I enter the light and leave the dark,
Your dreams can't come true unless you fight
It results in extreme changes that will make your life right,
So... are you, ready to fight?

Empowering yourself means you must inspire the one
around you
Don't devour your hopes, your dreams and fire up the one
around you,
Give a voice to the one who doesn't have one
Let them shine with you as you show your true skin,
After all, self-love is unconditional
So stop wasting time on the forgotten past and focus on
your promising future.

Shannon Casey (16)
St Mark's High School, Warrenpoint

My Dog That Walks On All Fours!

I love my dog, he is a nice little fellow,
He follows me around and makes me feel mellow.
He always knows when I need him the most.
He cuddles to me, he is as warm as toast.
He is as fluffy as a golden sheep.
As scruffy as a baby kitten.
He has a beautiful smile that lights up his face.
He loves to play with his ball while going to the mall.
He lets me know when it's time to sleep.
He knows what schedule I often keep.
He does all his tricks in a row until he overflows.
He shows me love, I love him so.
He treats me with respect
And when he feels like I'm in danger, he barks to protect.
He is an amazing and shy little guy,
Always there when I'm happy and there when I cry.
When it's time for his walk, he is as happy as he can be,
Come on, hurry up, walk with me.
He gets me outside, enjoying the day,
Tossing a stick so he can play.

If I asked for a miracle, I could not ask for more,
Than my little dog that walks on all fours!

Victoria Rosinska (12)
The Cardinal Wiseman Catholic School, Greenford

Before To Now

During last year things turned crazy
And I've become very lazy
Sitting on my bed, watching my phone
Being in my room all alone
Homeschooling was just so boring
I just felt like exploring
It would feel like a dream come true.

Looking back at what I've done
Things have been very fun
Watching and playing all day round
Not playing on the chilly ground
But now school has just begun
I have to go and have some fun.

Looking back at what I've done
Going back to normal has just begun.

Now and next we will see
Where life will take me
Going through this hard time
I've decided to make this poem rhyme.

Lenisha
The Cardinal Wiseman Catholic School, Greenford

Finding Yourself

You know who you want to be,
But not who you are.

Life isn't about finding yourself,
Because that implies that you're missing.

Life is about slowly breaking off the wall you've built around
yourself.

Attempting to find yourself is an ignorant way of life,
For you will spend eternity searching for something that can
never be found.

The moment you start searching within,
Is the moment you realise that you have been looking for
who you should be,

But now who you are.

Ryan El Fata (13)
The Cardinal Wiseman Catholic School, Greenford

A Love Letter To Trees

Trees, they grant us life,
Wondrous and important.

They get cut down,
They stay silent,
They cry,
They stay vibrant.

We dishonour them every day,
Our help is urgent.
Let's change our world,
Let this be our arrangement.

Don't wait any more,
We can save these creatures,
Change our lives,
Become achievers.

Trees, they grant us life
And they grant us our home.

Maria Kietla (13)
The Cardinal Wiseman Catholic School, Greenford

Deep Down The Wood

Deep down in the woodland,
There come the noises of a strange band.
The breeze gives the smell of soil,
Making the place awful and spoilt.

A canopy in the colour of green,
Makes the place look extreme.
It makes a tremendous scene,
To those animals who live therein.

Tall trees stand like statues,
Like the guardians of the forest.
But they all have different values,
To be exclusively useful.

Nathan Rebello (11)
The Cardinal Wiseman Catholic School, Greenford

Our Planet Is Dying

Our planet is dying, we don't know how or when.
All we know is we have to save it before then.
Our planet is dying whether it's the ground, sea or sky,
If we don't help now we'll have to say goodbye.
Our planet is dying, these animals are real.
Although most of them become a meal.
Our planet is dying, we don't know how or when,
But if we don't save it soon we'll never see it again.

Olivia Thomas (11)
The Cardinal Wiseman Catholic School, Greenford

Football

Football is my world
Football is my dream
Football means everything to me.

The stars you have...
Salah, Rashford, Kane, Sterling,
Ronaldo, Messi
The football teams are some of the best...
Chelsea, Arsenal, Leicester, Manchester United and
Liverpool.

The new signings can be really good players -
Some of them are the dream of football.

Dream of football.

Liam Fox
The Cardinal Wiseman Catholic School, Greenford

Unstrung Heartstrings

To illustrate the fall of the heart
and even how you played your part.
Like a siren, she sang her song for my ears, I fell apart
whenever I heard her voice.
But now, I've built up my defences
carrying my heartstrings, unstrung, and defended.
But until the future, when our pride untangles,
the feelings fade out as we forget,
that it never will feel like it did once before.

Tobias Devitt (16)
The Cardinal Wiseman Catholic School, Greenford

Until We Meet Again...

All those special memories of you will always make me smile
If only I could say goodbye one last time
Then I could tell you all my worries, just like I used to
You looked after me like you were cradling me in your arms
to protect me
The fact that you are no longer here will always cause me
pain
But you're here forever in my heart
Protecting me
Until we meet again...

Sienna Barry (12)
The Cardinal Wiseman Catholic School, Greenford

Earth

When I look down I often see
strange little creatures looking up at me,
through a telescope, they look with their eye,
they marvel at me in their sky so high.

I wonder how they see me from far away
am I so pretty as their planet during the day?
So interesting it is with its green and blue
oh Earth, am I as pretty as you?

Emilia Ciskal (12)
The Cardinal Wiseman Catholic School, Greenford

Poppies

Poppies, poppies on the green field
Where soliders' hands are on their shield.
William Harold fighting for the king,
Fighting on the green ring.

Poppies, poppies on us now,
To remember people's deaths right now.
People bowing on 11th November,
To stand a minute's silence now.

Lorreginus Uthayakumar (13)

The Cardinal Wiseman Catholic School, Greenford

My Crazy Neighbourhood

I live in number three
with my kind family.

In number one
lives Mrs Fun.

In number two
lives Mr Kangaroo.

In number four
lives Mrs Elor.

In number five
lives Mr Fright.

That's the end of my story,
Come back when I'm taller.

Maja Sarzalska (11)
The Cardinal Wiseman Catholic School, Greenford

About A Girl

I have a story
About a girl
A girl with skin like pearls and a mind like no one else's
A girl who doesn't know who she is
A girl who signs up to a race
The race of life

So the girl gets put far away
Away from many of the others
But the girl still triumphs more
More than the people in front

The girl finds a girl
Friends
And then finds a guy
After the two had split
And the girl gets pushed back some more
But she will not give in

She finally reaches the end
In relief
And grins in glee
The girl did it
She didn't give in
And lives the rest of her life happily.

Dylan Romeo (13)
The Holmewood School, Barnet

To A Dark, Dark Girl Aged 13

Along the shattered road
She stands proud and tall
Whilst they talk her down

Along the shattered road
They whisper and talk
Yet she will not let it in

She loves her dark, long, thick hair
The way her full lips look when she smiles

Along the shattered road
She stands proud and tall
What they say doesn't get into her head.

Maryan
The Holmewood School, Barnet

Just Because...

Just because you're black
You're cut no slack
Waiting for the chequered flag
Hoping for no more segregation without a snag.

Just because you're a woman
You're made to stay in the kitchen
Cleaning the house for hours
Made to feel like a maid in your own home.

Just because you're gay
You're made to stay away
Touched a guy
And gotta live with it.

Just because you're a lesbian
You're made to feel like a freak
Told you're meek
Told you're weak.

Just because you're poor
Made to live with fear
Living on the street
Getting cold feet.

Just because you're old
You feel cold
Disregarded, disrespected, disabled.

Just because you're a rugby player
Made to act strong
Made to put yourself through hell and back
Made to keep yourself holed up inside.

Just because you're an F1 driver
Expected to be fearless going into every turn
Expected to put your body on the line
Made to push yourself to the limit.

Just because you're you
Push yourself to the limit
Never give up
Fight to the final whistle
You are you.

You are as good as anyone
You are you
You are undefeatable.

Michael Goode (13)
The JCB Academy, Rocester

It Isn't That Great

If I could change anything for a day
I'd be confident to step up and say
The intention to support
Change and contort
The image we are giving ourselves
Through man-made change and hate.
Needless talk and debate
What can we hope for?
It isn't that great

However, there is something we can do
Helping our planet and keeping it green and blue
Preserving peace and making amends
To help the world and to get new friends
And with the rubbish that gets thrown
Turning poor fish to skull and bone
We should help them out and clear it up
To prevent our world becoming as worthless as dust
Otherwise it isn't that great to be there

But, really, it is a great place to be
With sprawling suburbs and beautiful trees
All we need to do is honour our luck
And prevent ourselves to be stuck
In this situation of climate change
And turn our world back and rearrange

The ways the Earth used to be
To keep those oceans, and keep those trees
Because then, it would be that great.

Archie Milward (13)
The JCB Academy, Rocester

Empowered

As we fight for our name,
We stand in a hall full of fame,
All alone, deep and enthroned,
With people named on a headstone,
All because they achieved their goal.

Power abuse by the law,
George Floyd put to the floor,
Black or white, we're still the same,
All the others put in shame,
Have you ever seen a white person be treated the same?

We all stand for our rights,
But not all can be right,
We can stand our ground,
And never have to fight,

Locked away for two years straight
Everyone is down and in a bad state
Looking depressed
Had no experience with all the rest

Making it awkward and not being the nicest
People turning racist, not really caring

Lost in a room
Full of darkness and despair

Nowhere to go
No light to spare
We see a keyhole with a bit of light
See a forest full of life
Kingdom full of peace and unity
A world ahead is made with immunity.

Preston Daniels (14)

The JCB Academy, Rocester

There's Only One Me

Why am I the way I am?
I wish I was one of those pretty girls
The ones that don't give a damn

I wish and I wish to stop feeling like this
Can I just not care at all
Tying to feel good again, I just feel small

A thousand voices howling in my head
I just back into the corner, lie there and cry
I keep listening and listening, hiding from them in my bed

I can't stop thinking about this, I couldn't
You can't just stop listening to them, you shouldn't
But you won't listen to them anymore, you wouldn't
You wouldn't, you wouldn't, you wouldn't

I am the way I am
I love the way I'm one of those pretty girls,
And no, I don't give a damn

I love that I feel good about myself
I don't care at all
Helping others feel good about themselves, help them not
feel small.

Milly Davies (13)
The JCB Academy, Rocester

Don't Let...

Don't let people say you couldn't,
Don't let them say you wouldn't,
Because they won't let you fly,
But that doesn't mean you can't reach for the sky.

Whether you're black, you're white, you're rich, you're poor,
Don't let opportunity walk away from the door,
Because we make opportunity happen, it doesn't come much,
But when it does we take it and nurture it, make it something so we aren't stuck with anything,

You can get shot down, you can fall,
But still, try to come out of it all,
Because life has to get worse to get better,
Maintain hope there will be that letter,

The past is the past, let's focus on the future,
Our ancestors' mistakes won't be ours,
We don't take from each other,
We fight with the other for equality.

Elliot Collins (14)
The JCB Academy, Rocester

Tomorrow

Through struggle, day and night
There is nothing to stop us, still we fight
Because through sadness and sorrow
There will still always be tomorrow

Bring me down, try if you can
But no matter what, I have a plan
From Japan, all the way to Morocco
There will always be tomorrow

In the darkness there is light
A hope, a dream, for which we can fight
Because while they may all look down below.
There is still tomorrow

We work hard and make progress
They can't bring us down, we will never rest
This makes our beliefs shine and glow
Because it is now nearly tomorrow

Though I may stand alone, no support behind me
I will stand up, with my beliefs and my family
We struggle and battle, we go with the flow
As the sun rises we can see it in the distance, we can see
tomorrow.

Charlie Giraldo (13)
The JCB Academy, Rocester

What Was It Like?

What was it like, when a tree could grow as tall as a
building?
When our fields were full of flowers
instead of pest-killing powders.
How could you let it become like this is forever confusing?

What was it like, when the stars could shine bright?
When they weren't drowned in the city light.
When the air we breathed was fresh and clean,
but now we wear masks because it is suffocating? What a
dream.

What was it like, when fish could swim freely in lakes, ponds,
even the sea
instead of our murderous rubbish bobbing like a buoyancy?
When kids would run around, read books, climb trees
but now their eyes are glued on useless screens.

Life sounds great when the Earth was alive,
so why won't you listen when I ask you to help me get it
back to what it was like?

Cara Weir (13)
The JCB Academy, Rocester

Empowerment

Empowerment is just a phrase
But if used wrong, it can turn into a craze
It can make you scream and shout
But people may use it for clout

Empowerment can be dangerous if used wrong
Some people may even shout and scream different songs
If you are mean or somehow green, people may scream that
you're just in the wrong and that they are right but that
would change overnight

People may feel engaged but really, they are enraged
People may feel empowered but in reality, people are just in
denial and then they run a mile
People may not understand but then people are as flexible
as a strand
Then it may get bad and then your family may be sad

To end this craze, people must understand that time and
effort is how to get fame
Now it's time to get a new frame.

George Hearson-McCarthy (14)
The JCB Academy, Rocester

If You Love Her...

If you love her she will be all you need,
If you love her she will occupy your dreams.

If you love her you want her protected,
If you love her you know she's perfected.

If you love her you'll acknowledge her wishes,
If you love her you'll give her lots of kisses.

If you love her there's no need to wait,
If you love her why should you hesitate?

If you love her set the message free,
And if she loves you she'll smile and gleam.

But if she doesn't, it's okay to cry and shout,
But not for too long, you've still got a life to figure out.

So wipe your tears and shed your skin,
Because if you loved her you'll do the right thing.

Go for it...

Jensen Wray (14)
The JCB Academy, Rocester

You Empower Me, I Empower You

It's all about courage, speaking out
Becoming stronger; more confident
But doing it with clout.

You empower me
I empower you.

It's all about society, it's me and you
Claiming our rights
Is what we should do.

You empower me
I empower you.

It's all about learning and being a team
Free to be true
Is living the dream.

You empower me
I empower you.

It's all about people from every race
The old and the young
Empowered with grace.

You empower me
I empower you.

It's all about choice and having belief
Being broken and beautiful
And fighting through life's grief.

You empower me
I empower you.

George Bolton (14)
The JCB Academy, Rocester

Empowered

I've empowered people far and wide,
My moments have caused defeat,
They fill me with such pride,
With a ball at my feet,
And no way of getting beat,
I'll empower how you feel on the inside.

I empower you using sound and a beat,
And I'll help you rise from the jaws of defeat,
It makes you feel like you're on a joy ride,
With rhythm at my ears,
And a rhyme at my tone,
I'll empower you with a microphone.

I'll empower you using paper in a book,
The words will trap you in an adventure,
That's why they call it a hook,
With a pen at my hand,
And paper in my vision,
I'll empower you with a paragraph that was written with precision.

Harry Mills
The JCB Academy, Rocester

Social Injustice

Our planet's in need.
A place where we live and breathe,
But first to succeed
We can't leave pollution.

We see injustice in the streets,
They choose to ignore it and stay in their seats.
Minorities villainised, but it's all deceit,
Something we need to defeat.

The ozone is breaking
But what risks are we taking?
People say we have a solution,
But all we see is pollution.

Some children are dying
And there is no point denying
'Cause healthcare is expensive
And minimum wage is just offensive.

But now it's all up to us.
The truth or the lies.
It's what we have to discuss
So we have to stand up and rise.

James Caulfield (13)
The JCB Academy, Rocester

Dear Dad

Dear Dad
I thank you for what you do
For always helping me, no matter how busy I may have
made you

You held my hand when I was weak
You protected me from the monsters that creak
Dried my eyes when they began to weep

You made me feel wanted when no one else did
You stuck by me when no one else would
I thank you for sharing your kindness and wisdom
For waiting after school when I was young

Taking me home, cooking me dinner
You will always be my greatest winner

One day you must go
That day will be full of pain and sorrow
But by then I hope you will know,
How much you helped
When my young, damaged heart you began to sew.

Maisy Loughlin (15)
The JCB Academy, Rocester

There Is Something We Can Do

Do you agree people need to be free
Or do you disagree?
People have the right to be happy whether you like it or not
They have a life, maybe a bit less than you do
There is something we can do
All we need is you
So don't just there doing nothing
Help, 'cause at the minute we are doing nothing
Help someone out who may be in need
But you still do nothing however much they plead
This is our choice, no one else's
Donate some money to help those in need
We need you to help us
Please don't make a fuss
We need you
There is something we can do.

Olivier Dodge (15)
The JCB Academy, Rocester

Living Your Life

You only have one life, live it to the fullest,
Don't play it safe, jump at opportunities,
It's your life, live it.

Don't waste your life,
Fly free like a bird,
We all have different journeys,
And challenges on the way.

We all live our lives differently but live for a common goal,
Whether that be starting a family or making your fortune,
No matter what we choose we all head towards the same
special place,
A special place where we can finally claim our reward for
our life.

But until then,
It's your life, live it.

Daniel Farrington (14)
The JCB Academy, Rocester

Stop Comparing You

Stop comparing your looks,
Your wealth,
Your popularity,
Stop comparing you.

Everyone is different,
No one is the same,
Make your own achievements,
Don't suffer in pain,
Stop comparing you.

They may seem happy, they may seem perfect,
But how do you know?
They would be depressed,
They would be lonely,
Stop comparing you.

You may be thirty,
Without a fancy car or a big house,
You may not have the lavish lifestyle,
But you are you,
Stop comparing you.

Daniel Peart (13)
The JCB Academy, Rocester

Reaching The Goal

I get given the ball, I knock it past one, knock it past another one,
I am one on one and then I see my old self in the goal,
A toddler walking towards me, I just don't know what to do!

I have worked hard for this,
I can't slip now,
I'm just going to shoot,
It's better safe than sorry.

Yes, I scored,
I'm so happy,
I see myself,
What have I done!

I feel bad,
I have no emotions,
I see crying, he looks so sad,
Everything suddenly went in slow motion.

Zak Kirvan (13)
The JCB Academy, Rocester

You Will Be Happy Again

Dear younger self, you will be happy,
Your eyes will twinkle again, in the lights,
Your smile will smile again when you see him,
You will be happy again.

The toxic friends will end,
You're finally two months clean,
The suicidal thoughts will fade,
You will be happy again.

When you meet him, you know he's the one,
The only one to make you happy,
The smiles and hugs, your love,
You will truly be happy.

Rebecca Gomm (14)
The JCB Academy, Rocester

Empowerment

Empowerment is living out of limits
Living to what you can do
Not what you're told you can do.

Empowerment is where you're in charge
Of what you want and can do
Not what you don't want to do.

Empowerment is becoming confident
Becoming stronger
And claiming your life.

Empowerment is in your everyday life
So there's no escaping it
Just accept the empowerment.

Caleb Dutton (15)
The JCB Academy, Rocester

Be Yourself

You are yourself.
Who else can you be?
You can't be anybody else
So set your goals free.

If you could be anyone, who could you be?
You should choose to be free.
Free from all the craziness in the world.
You should choose to be you.

You may see things people can't see.
You are you, keep it that way.
Every single day is a new day.
Don't let your dreams fade away.

Luca Mastroianni (13)
The JCB Academy, Rocester

My Uncle

My uncle was never full of dread,
He always got up and out of bed,
My uncle never wore a frown,
Even when things were seeming down.

My uncle always did his best,
Even when he was put to the test,
My uncle was always glad,
And was never, never bad.

My uncle inspired me,
To be the best that I can be,
Even if sometimes I failed,
My uncle never, never bailed.

Leon Chylinski
The JCB Academy, Rocester

Empowerment

No food, no water, no protection
The governments are in neglection
With people dying and crying.

But with hope, they try to succeed, to get a better life
With everyone leaving for their lives
The ones who survived were the ones who thrive.

With inequality between women and men
Which makes their abilities be crushed
And being hushed with no vote or rights.

Charlie Beardmore (13)
The JCB Academy, Rocester

Broken Family

When your family is broken so is your heart.
When your parents are apart it is hard but we fight it.
If it hurts we come back.
However difficult it is we conquer it.
It will always bring you down but we get back up.
As much as your heart sinks we must rise up again.
We must fight the pain that gives us great misery,
We always fight back and conquer it.

Jack Culverhouse (13)
The JCB Academy, Rocester

You Are You

You are a butterfly
Your colours are your personality
Your wings have the power to set you free
You are you.

You are a phoenix
You keep getting put down
But you will rise from the ashes
You are you.

You are a unicorn
You are filled with love and beauty
You have magic within you
You are you.

Jessica Nadin (13)
The JCB Academy, Rocester

Trolls

Dear past me,
When did the trolls start coming out from under the bridge?
When did they pop up in our social media feeds?

Dear past me,
They may be giant, monstrous and hostile
But you can face them.

Dear past me,
They are frightening but not all powerful.
You can, and will, use your magic to defeat them.

Daisy Hennah (14)
The JCB Academy, Rocester

Darkness Is Coming

As the dark rose over me
And brought me down
I didn't put on a frown
As evil tried to make me sad
I just fought away the bad.

As the darkness kept coming back
They didn't harm me, not even a crack
So if darkness wants to play it rough
I will stay strong and tough.

Ethan Gadsby (13)
The JCB Academy, Rocester

Inspiration

You give me help when I need it,
Inspire me to do the right thing,
You gave me a home,
You are there when I need you,
You are there when family die,
You are and always will be there,
The person who inspires people to do right.

Gethin Richards (13)
The JCB Academy, Rocester

I Am Me

I am a lion stalking my prey.
I am an Xbox, controlling the players.
I am a pop song repeating my tune.
I am a sofa, relaxing all day.
I am a house, strong and stable.
I am a football player scoring the winning goal.
I am me!

Callum Hughes (13)
The JCB Academy, Rocester

Thank You

He looks after the environment
He proves everyone wrong
And for that, he deserves a thank you.

He gives the animals a voice
He looks after their homes
And for that, he deserves a thank you.

Jayden Brewer (13)
The JCB Academy, Rocester

Animal Testing

You want to look pretty,
but what does it cost?
So many animals' lives are lost.

Animals suffer to make our skin gleam.
Nobody cares or hears their screams.

Bred for testing, not seeing the light of day.
Would you send your pet to live this way?

Burnt, injected and crammed in a cage
for us to look beautiful, never to age.

People protest about animal abuse,
but nothing changes so what's the use?

Testing still happens despite all the bans.
In 2022, there's still blood on our hands.

With no animal testing, how kinder life would be.
So choose cosmetics labelled cruelty free!

Tazmin Maarman (12)
Wollaston School, Wollaston

YOUNG WRITERS INFORMATION

We hope you have enjoyed reading this book – and that you will continue to in the coming years.

If you're the parent or family member of an enthusiastic poet or story writer, do visit our website **www.youngwriters.co.uk/subscribe** and sign up to receive news, competitions, writing challenges and tips, activities and much, much more! There's lots to keep budding writers motivated!

If you would like to order further copies of this book, or any of our other titles, then please give us a call or order via your online account.

Young Writers
Remus House
Coltsfoot Drive
Peterborough
PE2 9BF
(01733) 890066
info@youngwriters.co.uk

Join in the conversation!
Tips, news, giveaways and much more!